june 22

july 22

cancer

WHITE STAR PUBLISHERS

contents

Text by
Patrizia Troni

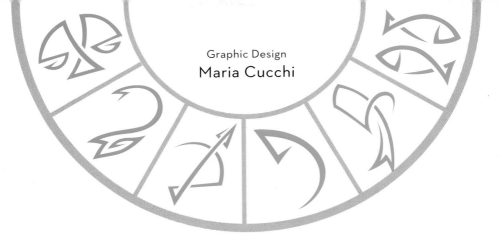

Graphic Design
Maria Cucchi

Character and Temperament

Cancer's is ruled by the Moon and their character acquires connotations that are, for the most part, lunar, which indicates exceptional sensibility, both in a positive and negative sense. Cancers hear and grasp everything, and filter everything through their hearts. But, it is precisely this capacity to amplify vibrations from their surroundings that sometimes makes them suffer. Just a couple of words might be enough to hurt them. Their highly delicate and hypersensitive souls need to withdraw into a shell, find a familiar, warm and safe shelter where they can be protected from a rude world. Cancer's character is lunar, due to a need to find peace and harmony, to take shelter in an almost dream-like place where their imagination can flourish softly and slowly be allowed to grow. For a Cancer, imagination is not mere fantasy, a daydream, an escape from reality and from the tension provoked by a barbarous world. No, for a Cancer, imagination is the very creation of reality, the possibility to intervene in an almost magical way, to rebuild and transform everything they dislike in the real world.

This explains some of their temporary withdrawals away from the 'real world', moments that alternate with cheerful moods when they become as brilliant and luminous as a full Moon – genial, creative and exceptionally fascinating.

Cancers are the sweetness of a tranquil heart that, since childhood, have lived on warm affection, which is more fundamental for them than for those born under other signs, in order to have a well-balanced character. Cancers are associated with everything pertaining to the magic of eternal childhood, and indeed, they always evince an undertone of innocence and enchanted purity, as if their reality were viewed through the eyes of a child.

But, this mythical childhood is also analogous to memory, as if a part of them always wanted to return to that period, when everything was pristine and clear-cut. That is why Cancer is also the sign of dreams, which are nothing more or less than the memory of a recurring past emotion and whose deep knowledge conceals the secret of being truly happy in the present.

While it is true that Cancers have an inexhaustible need for tenderness, it is also true that very few are as sweet and tender as Cancers. They are gracious and kind, always ready to put themselves on the same wavelength as others with the utmost delicacy. And, just as they are attentive to other's needs, they expect to be treated with the same gentility. Cancers are adamantly opposed to anyone entering, in an overbearing and intrusive manner, that subtle circle that is their sphere of identity. They dislike intrusions of any kind and are quite efficient at filtering and keeping at a safe distance those they consider unable to understand and, above all, to 'feel'.

Cancers are not exactly extroverts, although an ascendant of the Fire or Air elements is enough to make them extraordinarily communicative. On the other hand, all this does not mean that they are introverts or fragile or weak either. Quite the contrary. They know exactly what they want and are, usually, able to get it by means that might not be immediately noticeable. Their actions are not explosive, sensational, or aggressive, but are tenacious and their primary objective is to gain a 'safe haven' where true affection and feeling can rule supreme. In this sense, for Cancers, the family is a fundamental value, and Cancer parents are among the most attentive and intensely loving in the entire Zodiac.

Love and Passion

8 Cancer

Cancers adore love in all its forms. From the rapid, volatile version triggered by a fleeting glance, to profound, constant, eternal love that is wrapped up in itself like the petals of a rose, developing over the years with attachment that is intense and yet capable of drifting sweetly into domestic routine.

Cancers like tender, sweet love with its kisses, caresses and other manifestations of affection, as well as overwhelming, passionate love that is like a maelstrom, a swirling torrent that overflows and spreads all over.

Cancers like both poetic, magical, very delicate love and secret, obscure love. For them, love is fundamental and they know how to season it in many different ways. Love is what captivates and enraptures them more than anything else, triggering the imagination and daydreams. And, just as Cancers are able to share and cherish, moment after moment and gesture after gesture, the daily existence of your only love, so you are able to liberate an extraordinary, constant flow of invention that achieves remarkable peaks of quality even from an erotic standpoint. The atmospheres you create, the stories you propose, the magical places where you take your partner, all enhance your Eros with very spicy

flavors that are unimaginable for those who observe you from outside, where you seem to be so tranquil, helpless and timid.

Yes, you are timid, but only at first sight. In the tangled matters of love, you are certainly not the types who arrive with a flourish, sensationally attracting and bewitching. Cancers may adore the fleeting game of seduction and be quite capable of giving explicit demonstrations of their feeling, but in reality they let the true heart that gives shape to great love, express itself very slowly. This is because it is a prudent heart, wrapped in an aura of exceptional delicacy and sensitivity, and when it falls in love it wants to take into account a series of qualities that the other person must have, a combination of intense affection, a lively mind and desirable and desiring feeling.

Another fundamental aspect of the question is the manifestation of love on the part of the other person. As a Cancer, you enjoy being 'courted', you like it when someone manages to pass beyond that defensive bulwark you sometimes place around yourself. For you, the choice to establish a romantic relationship does not depend solely on intense sensual pleasure and eroticism. What really moves your heart beyond the game of seduction – a field in which you are a world authority, by the way – is the effective assurance and certainty that you will be enveloped and protected by true love that will remain strong, even when you are absent, absorbed in other matters, moody, or surly. In your opinion, love is the realization of great harmony that delicately and slowly offers you a clear answer to your infinite desire to be loved and the need for security, without the occasional painful spurts of the heart.

In a couple, you often reveal your childish side. Here the male seeks maternal protection from his mate, a mother figure who will constantly reassure him, while his female counterpart wants the protection of a strong male figure that can lead her with constancy and resolution. But, these projections are overturned: the Cancer male is able to be available and protective and the Cancer woman, who was so fond of being a child, proves to be solid and invincible. You don't like quarrelsome love stories that transform this sentiment into a battle or even a war. You are hurt by cold, detached behavior, routine that leads to a lack of true empathy. If something goes wrong in your relationship, if you feel hurt or offended, or if loves turns out to be a one-way street, you do not downplay this but immediately go to the heart of the problem, because you cannot bear being in a state of miserable doubt.

How to Hook a Cancer and How to Let Them Go

If a Cancer attracts you, you must bear in mind that their great sensitivity is made up of both fragility and strength. Cancers find it difficult to express their feelings clearly and openly, so that winning their hearts is not easy and, usually, not immediate. It won't take centuries, but a bit of patience and perseverance will be necessary. Cancer think with their heart, speak with their heart and listen to their heart. In order to hook them you must make a breakthrough in this area, conquer the stronghold in which they hide their doubts, timidity and ancestral fears. In order to woo a Cancer woman you must be sweet and, at the same time, sturdy, easy-going and obliging yet strong, both imaginative and practical. You should also tell her you love her at least three times a day, place tender notes on her pillow. She needs to be certain that her changing moods are understood and accepted without you being either invasive or detached. A word of warning: do not make the mistake of confusing her blushes and hesitation with fragility. By doing so, you will, inevitably, become entrapped by her fascination. In order to woo a Cancer male, double those massive doses of sweetness. He should never be left alone and you must always make your presence felt. You should not become discouraged if, during the early phases, you seem to be taking one step forward and three steps back. Simmering the relationship slowly is his way of testing you. He should be reassured by strong, protective, sweet, practical and efficient femininity. A Cancer male wants a tender yet solid woman by his side who can bear the weight of daily problems for him, something he would appreciate quite a lot.

It doesn't take much to send Cancers off course. Slight changes in the way they are loved is enough to put them in crisis. If you want to leave a Cancer, you must not be harsh or cruel. The rupture in your relationship should be sugared quite a lot: tell them that you are hurt more than they are by the separation and that they will always have an important place in your heart.

Compatibility with Other Signs

The most compatible signs for Cancer are Pisces, Taurus and Virgo who understand Cancer's moodiness. These other signs bring fine professional synergy and instant common feelings. There is deep understanding with Scorpios as well, but you must show them your claws, impose your will and not appear too fragile if you don't want to be the weak link in the relationship. As regards compatibility with the Fire signs, it is total with Leo, but less stable and immediate with Aries and Sagittarius, who are too bold and frenetic for Cancer's need for tranquility. Proud and generous Leo, on the other hand, provides you with a lot of energy and they like your being a mixture of sweetness, timidity and arrogance, futile withdrawal and bursts of vitality.

Capricorns are poles apart from you regarding mentality and approach to life. Theoretically, there is very little understanding between the two of you, but solid and fruitful friendships, as well as intensely passionate relationships, may be established if this difference turns into a strong attraction between two strong temperaments: Cancer gains support and security from a Capricorn, who in turn assimilates the other's sweetness and creativity.

Cancers like formal beauty, a poetic vein mixed with the crystalline rationality of Libra, but do not agree with its mental rigidity and domineering attitude. You can have pleasant and invigorating vacations with an Aquarius, while, in regards to professional or family matters, things are much less invigorating because the inconstant and unpredictable nature of Aquarius has a destabilizing effect on you. Geminis are extroverts and always on the move, while you are introverted and lazy. Here, too, we have two different temperaments that can complement each other, leading to benefits on both sides. The great lake of Cancer sensitivity becomes an ocean when it meets another Cancer; the result can be a galactic love story, the same dream-like pauses, the same need for support and the same oversensitivity. A true idyll.

Cancer Profession and Career

Many people say that Cancers are lazy loafers and that they often take too much time to finish everything. In fact, when what they are doing really enthuses them and goes hand in hand with their desires, they become resistant, tenacious, indefatigable and constant, more than any other sign. There are sign personalities for whom work is the most important thing in their lives, and they perform it routinely and mechanically, much like robots. But, Cancers are not robots; they cannot separate their soul from what they are involved in. And, in their profession as well, they never forget or neglect their soul, and their soul does not forget their heart.

The Cancer workplace must be harmonious, where everyone gets along and where arguments, hard or frosty feelings, conflicts and unhealthy competition do not exist. Cancers are good-hearted, and just as they treat their colleagues cordially they want them to be warm and friendly.

A Cancers job must not be a form of punishment or suffering, something coercive. Very little is needed to create the right atmosphere harmony and true friendship among the workers. Lacking this, Cancers isolate themselves and prefer to work alone, in solitude, silence and calm. Which is not a bad idea, because they end up being more productive than others, despite their slower pace, oscillating rhythm, absences and suspensions.

When the atmosphere is optimum your lazy or idle appearance gives way to that of a tireless worker, a jackhammer, a force of nature; you dive into your work and into the analogy Cancer has with waterways; you become a raging torrent that overwhelms everything until the goal has been reached. However, your superiors must not suffocate or stress you, be constantly on your back, prodding you harshly and brusquely. Otherwise, you will end up not meeting your deadlines, and when gripped with anxiety everything may become more difficult. In the field of work, you are brilliant both as an executor and as an entrepreneur. The law you obey is not only that of convenience, profit, or of the brutal economy; it is the law of the heart. If you love something and the goal you aspire to arouse your passion, then there is no obstacle that can block you, you become a tsunami.

Your remarkable sensitivity makes you an excellent manager, because you never treat people as if they were objects who are there only to produce, but are always attentive to the emotional state of the group. When a work environment is harmonious it is ten times

✿　✿　✿　✿　✿　✿　✿

more productive, and many companies have grasped this concept. Thus, you make a perfect director, always appreciated and well liked.

As an employee, it is important that your superiors be both gentle and understanding with you and know how to create that feeling that instills trust and confidence in you. Then, you become the best of the group, demonstrating great loyalty as well as becoming a driving force fundamental to the entire team. Many Cancers are teachers, company managers or supervisors, as well as art collectors, archaeologists, antique dealers, plumbers, taxi drivers and bakers. Cancer has a connection with everything relating to homes, which has produced a large number of Cancer architects, interior designers, and cabinet-makers. Your inventive flair and genius is also expressed in the field of advertising, especially as creative advertisers rather than graphic artists. The correspondence Cancer has with every form of literature has produced great authors and poets, some outstanding examples being Leopardi, Proust, Kafka, Hesse and Hemingway. The exceptional creativity typical of Cancer is also to be seen in such utopian and visionary geniuses of science as Nikola Tesla.

How Cancer Thinks and Reasons

Cancer is one of the most intuitive signs of the Zodiac. Whatever their level of intelligence or cultural background, they 'see' and 'feel' everything at a glance, grasping that invisible essence that reveals the truth, in the minutest detail. They are not enchanted by fine words with no purpose, and while it is true that certain rigorous attitudes or lines of reasoning strike them there and then, their judgment depends only partly on the logical truth that has been stated. Their heart has already understood it all. Just a facial expression or a detail of body language to understand what another person really thinks, and they have already decided how to deal with the other person.

Cancers are not masters of cold logic, or of calculation, or of absolute certainty and few philosophers have been born under Cancer. Cancers are masters of imagination, of visionary synthesis that grasps the essence of a matter in an instant. At certain moments you might seem to be absent-minded, distracted, intimidated, but never fanatical and rash in any discussion, because all you need is a concept, an idea, and your imagination gallops off, perhaps even losing the thread of the conversation. The truth is, since you immediately understand the truth of another's heart, rigorous thought is relegated to a secondary role. Yours is an intelligence of the heart par excellence, what psychologists for years have been calling emotional intelligence.

This does not mean that you do not have 'your' logic. You know quite well where you want to go. In this sense your intelligence is made manifest more in flashes of inspiration or sudden intuition, which may arrive unexpectedly, surprising and wrong-footing others. Your thought is a flash of lightning that arrives suddenly in the form of a transparent, pure and innocent truth that amazes others because, in an instant, you have skipped all the processes of mechanical reasoning in which many proudly rational people thread their way for an interminable length of time. You present the truth like a shot; it is always expressed delicately, almost whispered, but is exceptionally incisive and enlightening.

Cancers are also moody when expressing their opinions and thoughts; there are days when they seem enchanted, dazed, and almost detached from the context. But, in truth, they note everything and their unconscious, which is quite rich and always operates in a dream-like dimension, suddenly provides the connection that reveals the truth. At times it would seem that you do not want to understand or that you are 'playing dumb', while actually their unconscious has seen everything. Your soul is more that of a poet than a cold accountant. Cancers are rarely rational, and when they are, it is because they force themselves to be so. Their thought is best expressed with persons who are pure of heart, especially children, whom they understand and with whom they establish a marvelous dialog, often in the form of a fable or story. This is the reason why Cancers make high-quality teachers.

It may be that, as regards classical reasoning, you are a bit slow and need time to think things out, that you may seem to be somewhat enigmatic and unfathomable, and that those who seem to possess the absolute truth sometimes strike you. But, it is also true that, in the end, you are well aware of what your own truth is. You are frank and honest with yourself and have the lucid strategy to come up with an answer or opinion, perhaps when others least expect it.

Sociability, Communication

and Friendship

Cancer is not one of the most social signs of the Zodiac. You do not like noise and confusion, situations in which persons and personalities make their appearance and then disappear, in an instant, contexts in which only the image and form count. You are hardly concerned about appearances and are certainly not inclined to hop from one party or 'event' to another. Large groups are not in tune with your extraordinary sensitivity. You prefer to communicate with a few intimate friends, tête-à-tête, when the conversation, acquaintance and exchange of ideas slowly develop, ideally in a low voice and in a setting with soft lighting. You like dialogs, words that go directly to the heart, where sentiment and immediate empathy create the channel through which people meet and communicate. This does not mean that you are unable to get about in the world; on the contrary, you are well liked because of your gentle and harmonious behavior, your grace and charm that become sensitivity and profound understanding of others' feelings. You are neither cold and cerebral nor superficial persons who appreciate fleeting conversations. You lose interest in discussions of ideas or knowledge if the essential ingredient, the heart, is lacking. Banal, trite communication is not for you. On the other hand, you adore communication that is very intense, high-level, vibrant, and almost magical. Too much talk bores you and hubbub disturbs you. The vacuous nature of nondescript persons, whose conversation remains on a very superficial level, really irritates you.

Cancers are receptive to everybody and are anything but small-minded. Yet, in a way, their sociability could be called selective, since it keeps its distance from people who disturb their inner tranquility or who they instinctively sense are negative.

Their behavior with others rarely manifests a strong, extroverted ego. Cancers do not state directly, and prefer to suggest, to hint. And, the essence of your communication always transmits, between the lines, the need for emotional harmony and accord that they cannot do without. They move about on tiptoe, so to speak, but leave significant traces in all the people they meet.

Due to the connection that Cancer has with the past and with childhood, the friendships they established when young are those that remain for ever, partly because when they open their hearts – and, as we have seen, they do so very slowly – it stays wide open. Thus, for Cancers, friendship is something profound, since it is the result of a process of absolute selection. They dislike relationships that are created in a moment and end just as quickly. For Cancers, what counts most are deep, intense feelings that need no words in order to be understood.

You cannot tolerate overly exuberant people, the pushy ones who arrive unexpectedly at your house, the arrogant ones who impose their viewpoint and always want to teach you and preach to you. Unlike Zodiac signs, for you friendship is not based on, or prompted by, duty and convenience. It is nourished by long periods of close contact that alternate with periods of absence that take you back to solitude, which is sacred for you since it revitalizes you. In friendship, your lunar rhythm consists of moments of intense closeness and other phases during which you disappear entirely from circulation. Then, suddenly, memories prompt the triggering of past emotions and the need to feel the presence of that certain person; and you find them again, in that atmosphere of marvelous accord of which you have always had such fond memories.

When Cancer Gets Angry

All books and essays concerning astrological signs agree that Cancer is a sign of moodiness. Your mood changes more quickly than the phases of the moon. Without a doubt, you are moody, touchy and often unpredictable. Your golden rule is passive, receptive adaptation. Cancers, especially when fiery Mars, the luminaries or Pluto with favorable ascendants are lacking on your birth chart, do not like to struggle, and stay away from any form of competition. Cancers use the crab shell as a shield and prefer not to emerge to fight. But, should you do so, it is because something has really infuriated you. You have an infantile and touchy temperament, which means that you might be easily irritated, offended, and angered over things that others would disregard without thinking twice about it. A simple change in the tone of voice, a mere word or gesture, are enough to hurt your feelings and put you in a state of hostile silence. You are like extremely delicate crystal vases. In order not to disturb your oversensitive emotions, those near you must be masters of tact and sensitivity, understand from your mumbled phrases or changes of mood that they have said or done something wrong. However, this delicate disposition and amiable mildness must not be mistaken for weakness. Nor should others believe that there is no grit in your character. You may not like conflict, but you are quite capable of becoming inflexible, intransigent and harsh, and will have no qualms about ending a relationship with anyone or anything that has deeply hurt you. People who invade your privacy, invade your space, or are indelicate or indiscreet, make you very angry. The same is true of those who meddle in or want to change your status quo or habits, who want to separate you from what is most precious to you. Another thing that annoys you is having to provide explanations, make comprehensible what is already quite clear in your head, and being ridiculed for making a mistake. You are easily offended. Consequently, if you do make a mistake, a rebuke can come only from you yourself.

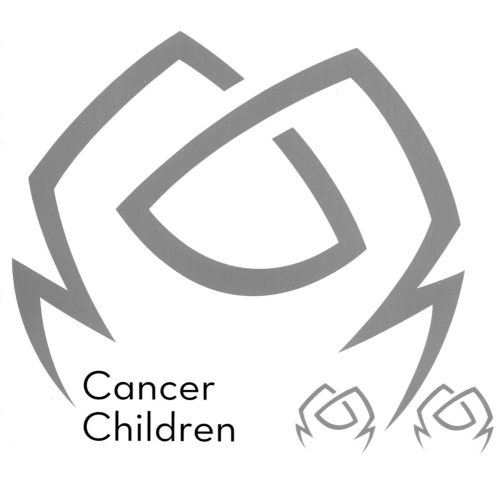

Cancer
Children

Cancer children are among the most sensitive in the Zodiac, as well as exceptionally ingenuous and impressionable. They absorb emotions and sensations like a sponge. Since they are so easily cut to the quick, their parents must be receptive and empathetic in order to understand their moods, while at the same time making sure not to be tyrannized by their whims and demands for attention and understanding. Cancer children have extremely sensitive antennae that are on the same wavelength as their parents' character. Should they discover a weak point they will take full advantage of it.

Avoid being too strict when they get into mischief. Their touchy, oversensitive nature, which amplifies emotions, might lead them to withdraw into their shell and become isolated. It is more advisable to appeal to the sensitivity and goodness of a heart that is naturally inclined to being sorry and to being apologetic. The emotional atmosphere in the family is essential for the children's education; in fact, negative experiences at home will beset them in their adult life. Both Cancer boys and Cancer girls identify themselves with, and seek the support of, their mother. They want shelter and comfort from their mother and approval from their father.

In order to overcome their natural laziness, it would be a good idea to put these children through their paces from their early childhood onwards in order to make them self-assured and purposeful. In order for these children to do their best at school, they must feel they are in a warm, non-competitive, family-type atmosphere with teachers who are neither brusque nor overbearing. They have an excellent memory; once they grasp something, they never let

it go. This gift of good memory is precious for their formal education, but these children tend not to try their best at school, where phases of apathy alternate with excessive enthusiasm. It is up to their parents to spur them on, follow their progress and lead them, without making their presence oppressive, and always bearing in mind that the children's rhythm must be respected and understood.

Music Associated

Although there are Cancers who like unrelenting, rhythmic, explosive, hard music, generally speaking, what you prefer most is enchanting, amazing, mellow, delicate music that expresses that sentimentalism which is then enhanced by your extraordinary and surprising imagination. For you, music must be sweet magic, a spell that transmits evocative echoes, possibly to a slow tempo and silver-toned melody, a companion that is never at high volume but synchronizes your being with the wavelengths of a heart that seeks serenity and wants to avoid the dull, cold aspects of everyday life. The music you listen to often contains poetry, ballads and songs with rather intimate and winning lyrics that are narrative and express your gift of storytelling, which is one of Cancer's exceptional qualities. Thus, we have the long, rather melancholic and 'maverick' stories narrated by Woody Guthrie, a master who greatly influenced Bob Dylan, as well as the somewhat psychedelic and electronic jazz of pianist Joe Zawinul, who

with Cancer

began his career with Miles Davis. Cancers have an extraordinary musical soul that, through careful guidance and constant application, can also produce great symphony orchestra conductors, such as Gustav Mahler (who was also a leading composer) and Claudio Abbado.

In the history of rock music, we must not forget Kris Kristofferson, Jeff Beck, Carly Simon, Deborah Harry, Carlos Santana or Cat Stevens. A world-famous Cancer is Ringo Starr, the Beatles percussionist: a silent, lunar presence, the one least noted in the great Liverpool quartet but, as critics acknowledged, one of the mainstays of the band. The instruments that correspond to Cancer, the first of the Water signs, are the viola d'amore and the harp.

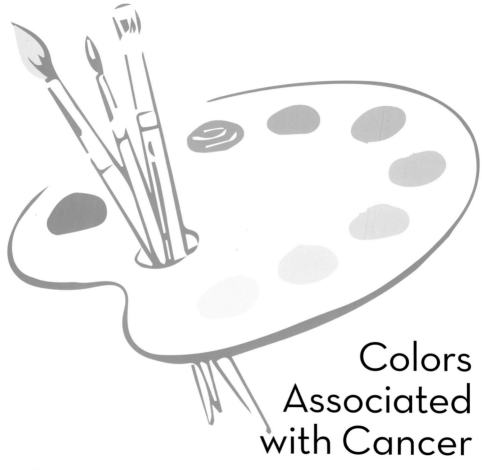

Colors
Associated
with Cancer

Look up at the sky, at your guiding 'planet' the Moon. Silver white, snow white, spectral white, brilliant white. In fact, white is Cancer's color. It is an ancient, pure, immaculate color, just like the essence of Cancer. A non-color color that symbolizes absolute silence, withdrawal into oneself, meditation, immaculate snow that covers everything and puts it at rest. A color associated with absence (think of such common expressions as 'white night' or sleepless night; and 'white flag', which stands for a truce or cessation of hostility) and with the soul, which is lily white before it sins. White evokes purity, serenity, inner peace, cleanliness, divine light. Priests' garments are white; among the Celts, the druids dressed in white; in Buddhism the halo and white lotus are associated with the Buddha's 'knowledge or wisdom fist' gesture. Sweetness, the magical magnetism that you transmit to others, the sensitivity with which you treat everything around you, are all symbolized by creamy white. This is also a perfect color for a romantic rendezvous and to be in empathy with another person.

You wear a milk white garment when you want to stay in your shell, protected from the confusion and chaotic pollution of the world or when you must put your life in order, pick up the pieces, as it were, or must curb a sense of inadequacy, the fear of not being able to face reality. This hue of white helps you to rid yourself of insecurity, tension and stress. You choose ivory white when you want to transform a difficult moment into a great opportunity for regeneration in order to show the world your enviable stamina. Snow white helps you to filter, with cool logic, the stimuli and sensations that arrive in an uninterrupted flow. And, you prefer pearly white when you must use your fascination as an invincible means of seduction and conviction.

Flowers
and Plants
Associated
with
Cancer

Cancer heralds the coming of summer. Wheat is a sea of gold in the fields, and luxuriant vegetation a flurry of scents and colors. Everything reveals the power and creative quality of nature. You connect this solar expansion and your lunar side with flowers such as *Mirabilis Jalapa* (beauty of the night or the four o'clock plant), whose inebriating scent always attracts moths and whose flowers open in the late afternoon; peonies (which the ancient Greek physician Thessalus stated had beneficial effects on lunatics); and the lotus, nasturtium, jasmine and hybrid petunia. You can decorate your home or office with cacti. Their sharp thorns disintegrate negative energy; furthermore, the cactus symbolizes your reserve and your need to keep your distance from anything that disturbs your sense of serenity.

Here are some flowers and plants associated with the three ten-day periods of Cancer.

First period (June 22-July 1): lilac (*Syringa Vulgaris*). In ancient times, it was believed that fairies and elves lived quite happily in this rustic shrub with sweet-smelling flowers. What you like about lilac is its pure white inflorescence, but its mauve flowers are also beneficial to and compatible with your ten-day period. Lilac protects you from excessive emotion and increases your capacity for reflection, which is surprisingly strong.

Second period (July 2-12): linden. Just as the fragrant flowers of linden trees provide bees with delicious nectar, so you, with typical grace, attract looks and desires. Use the essence if you want to enchant or even captivate with your words. A bath with linden alleviates insomnia and nervous states.

Third period (July 13-22): water lily. This is a lunar flower par excellence that was once thought to favor journeys, including mental ones with dreams and visions. The water lily symbolizes your candor, your need for withdrawal and silence. When melancholy strikes you, if you feel you are misunderstood or are unhappy, stressed out or disappointed, sit near a lake filled with water lilies, which will absorb everything that disturbs you and will make you tranquil.

Animals Associated with Cancer

Animals that are lunar, and hence influenced by the Cancer sign, are the chameleon with its changing colors, the deer, fallow deer and fawn, panther, hyena and cats, which dilate and contract the pupils of their eyes, just as the Moon appears to increase and decrease in size. Then, among the birds are geese, ducks, and the nightingale. But, the creatures that are most connected on a symbolic level with Cancer are the crab and crayfish. The summer solstice occurs during Cancer, the magical midsummer night, when the longest day is paired with the shortest night. Cancer was considered one of the two great gates of the Zodiac, the other being Capricorn. During the summer solstice, souls descended to earth through the Gate of Cancer, ready to be re-incarnated, while they re-ascended to heaven at the winter solstice through the Gate of Capricorn. Daytime begins to decrease at the summer solstice and the Sun, having reached its maximum declination, begins to 'bend backward'. The crab and crayfish, which walk backward and very slowly, symbolize the Sun apparently slowing down. They also symbolize the fickleness of Cancer, the difficulty you find in getting started, your tendency to let time slip by, to procrastinate, for an unseemly length of time, matters that you manage to solve in no time once you have decided to deal with them. Your love of home, in comfort with your habits and routine, living at a slow pace, also corresponds to the snail and, just like a snail, the slightest indication of intrusion makes you withdraw into your shell; your home is a refuge for you, a warm, cozy place where you can stay, shut off from the rest of the world. Other creatures connected to Cancer are the moth, which flies at night, and the glow-worm, which illuminates summer nights and dreams of love with its light. Then there is the octopus, the cuttlefish, the eel (if you find yourselves under pressure you slip away like an eel), the catfish and the torpedo ray.

Gemstones Associated with Cancer

As a Cancer, if you want to benefit from the power of gemstones and crystals, you should choose ones that are white, transparent, pearly, and moonlike. Certain ones are particularly connected to Cancer: selenite or moonstone, mother-of-pearl, pearls and rock crystal. As Cornelius Agrippa states in his *Occult Philosophy III* regarding stones under the power of the Moon, "Also the stone Selenite (*i.e.* Lunary), shining from a white body, with a yellow brightness, imitating the motion of the Moon, having in it the figure of the Moon which daily increaseth, or decreaseth as doth the Moon." A female stone par excellence, selenite was used by clairvoyants, who placed it on their forehead, or under their tongue, to foretell the future. Besides increasing sensory perception and the ability to see into the future, selenite protects those who travel at night and by sea. In fact, it was worn when one wanted to have a happy journey – and an even more felicitous return. But, it is also the stone of love and hope. It should be worn when you are searching for true love and do not want to have disappointing experiences. In ancient times, people believed that selenite would lose its brilliance if those who wore it were no longer in love or were involved in a relationship not worthy of the name 'love'. Gems that come from the sea, mother-of-pearl and pearls, make your spirit more luminous. Pearls should, preferably, be either white or cream-colored and should not be given as a token or pledge of love because they are associated with tears. But, when worn as mere ornaments, pearls maintain their beauty and youthful freshness, heightening your soft, voluptuous sensuality. Rock crystal gives you energy, strength and vitality. According to tradition, they stimulate introspection and favor movement toward the outside world. Finally, mention should made of the fact that the metal most compatible with Cancer is silver, so that your jewelry should be made of silver or at least white gold.

Best Food for Cancer

Cancer is a Water sign, nocturnal and feminine, and what is best for your delicate Cancer character, which often somatizes emotions and impressions, are delicate flavors, tending to be insipid rather than salty. Furthermore, while it is generally known that one should drink at least 1.5 liters of water every day, for you this healthy habit is an imperative. It must be water – still water, and plenty of it – rather than effervescent beverages and distilled spirits, beer and wine. As we saw earlier, you are impressionable and your problems, anxieties and insecurities tend to be somatized in your stomach. In cases of stomach cramps, heartburn, etc. it is advisable to drink a melissa or lemon balm herbal tea. Used since ancient times for nervous spasms and indigestion, lemon balm favors biliary secretion and natural digestion.

To flavor sauces and dishes in general, you should use onions and chives rather than garlic. Fish, whether freshwater or saltwater, must be a mainstay of your diet, especially eels, salmon, octopus, tuna and sardines, and oysters. While the, much vaunted, aphrodisiac properties of the oyster have not really been demonstrated, what is certain is that it has low calorie and fat content and is rich in omega-3, iron, zinc, copper and selenium. Another food to include in your diet is egg white, which is the color associated with your sign; unlike the yolk, it has no fat or cholesterol and is rich in water and protein.

Cancer is also associated with everything sweet. Sugar, cake and pastries, 'cotton candy', cream and candy are irresistible to you. You tend to add lots of sugar to your coffee and tea, along with a slice of cake, an éclair or a cream puff. If you have no health problems and are not overweight, you can delight your palate and follow your natural inclination. Otherwise, you must be judicious.

Myths
Associated
with Cancer

Cancer is nocturnal, feminine, creative and changeable, and is mirrored at a mythological level with all the mother and lunar goddesses, such as Isis, Cybele, Astarte and Ishtar. Above all, you identify yourself with the triple moon goddess – Selene, Hecate and Artemis – each of whose three phases reflects your personality.

You are Selene, the full moon, when you reveal your proud, self-assured, bewitching glance, so full of sensations and impressions; when you speedily immerse yourselves in even the most difficult of situations; when you give yourself over entirely to your imagination and transform even the ugliest thing into pure magic; and when you step out confidently into the world, opening the gates of your sensuality, radiating waves of fascination. You are Hecate when the Moon is black and you reveal your dark side; when you do not open up to others because the perceptions you defend are too precious and intimate; when you grasp the essence of things as if everything came to you without any effort; when you are totally absorbed in silent contemplation; and when you unleash the occult forces in your being and you become explosive, unpredictable, inexorable and ruthless.

You are Artemis when the Moon is waxing, and your self-confidence grows so much that it overflows and you succeed in achieving what you had thought was impossible; when you live your dreams while remaining concrete; and when you leave your comfortable shell and pass from a passive to an active state.

The connection between Cancer and the dream world refers to another myth, that of Morpheus, the son of Sleep and Night and the god of dreams. It was once believed that, during his nocturnal apparitions, Morpheus sent illusory suggestions and prophetic dreams to humans. "Those who dream by day are cognizant of many things which escape those who dream only by night," Edgar Allan Poe stated. Cancer dreams both during the day and during night.

Cancer Fairy Tale

Sleeping Beauty, written by Perrault, is perfect for Cancer. It is the story of a princess struck down by a cruel curse – that she will grow up beautiful and happy in her castle, but when she is sixteen years old, she is doomed to prick her hand with a spindle and to sleep, without dreaming, for 100 years, until she is awakened by the kiss of a prince. Sleep and the world of dreams make for the strongest connection between Cancer and this fairy tale. Cancers need to sleep, and crave sleep. You benefit greatly from long, deep sleep. For the Dalai Lama, a Cancer, "sleeping is the best meditation."

When the noises of the world upset you, when life knocks too violently on your door, when you are distressed, feel oppressed and saddened by thoughts, both big and small, you would like to fall into a sleep so deep that you would wake up 100 years later – perhaps thanks to a kiss from a handsome prince or beautiful princess, because, for you, love is like gold dust that illuminates life and makes it magnificent. It is not easy to win your heart, but the person who manages to do so will be rewarded a remarkably intense gift.

You adore kisses, both being covered with kisses and smothering those you love with kisses. Your lips are the sweetest in the entire Zodiac. Like the prince's kiss in the fairy tale, kisses from a Cancer revive, invigorate, reanimate, relieve and tonify. Because your kisses are languid, captivating and dreamlike, they unleash a chemical reaction that awakens the vital and sensual side of even the coldest and most misanthropic of partners. Sleeping Beauty, who falls asleep when she is an adolescent and is an adult when she awakens, symbolizes the great effort that many Cancers make when passing through the various phases of life. Adolescence, puberty, and adulthood: every period that changes the life cycle leaves its mark on a sensitive and emotional Cancer, a mark that, at times, is indelible.

PATRIZIA TRONI, trained at the school of Marco Pesatori, writes the astrology columns for Italian magazines *Marie Claire* and *Telepiù*. She has worked in the most important astrology magazines (*Astra, Sirio, Astrella, Minima Astrologica*), she has edited and written the astrology supplement of *TV Sorrisi e Canzoni* and *Chi* for years, and she is an expert not only in contemporary astrology, but also in Arab and Renaissance astrology.

Photo Credits

Archivio White Star pages 28, 34, 38; artizarus/123RF page 20 center; Cihan Demirok/123RF pages 1, 2, 3, 4, 14, 30, 48; Yvette Fain/123RF page 46; file404/123RF page 16 bottom; Olexandr Kovernik/123RF page 42; Valerii Matviienko/123RF pages 8, 12; murphy81/Shutterstock page 44; Igor Nazarenko/123RF page 40; Michalis Panagiotidis/123RF pages 20, 21; tribalium123/123RF page 16; Maria Zaynullina/123RF page 36

WS WHITE STAR PUBLISHERS

WS White Star Publishers® is a registered trademark
property of De Agostini Libri S.p.A.

© 2015 De Agostini Libri S.p.A.
Via G. da Verrazano, 15 - 28100 Novara, Italy
www.whitestar.it - www.deagostini.it

Translation: Richard Pierce - Editing: Norman Gilligan

ISBN 978-88-544-0966-8
1 2 3 4 5 6   19 18 17 16 15

Printed in China